The Voice of Small Business

Hard Times

Arthur Lee

Arthur Lee Books
Melbourne, Australia

Copyright © 2022 Arthur Lee
www.arthurlee.com.au

All rights reserved. No part of this book may be reproduced, or stored in a retrieval system, or transmitted in any form or by any means, electronic, mechanical, photocopying, recording, or otherwise, without express written permission of the publisher.

Every effort has been made to trace or contact all copyright holders. The publishers will be pleased to make good any omissions or rectify any mistakes brought to their attention at the earliest opportunity.

ISBN: 9798362294779
Imprint: Independently published

Arthur Lee
PO Box 161, Forest Hill VIC 3131
Australia
ABN: 29 172 617 138

Contents

An open wound 1
From eviction to success 3
Succeeding was a necessity..9
A risk that paid off 17
The success of a warm heart...23
Scaling the business to survive 29
Trial and error is a great teacher....................................35
On the brink of failure..41
Maths is all part of business..49
Failure as a badge of honor..55
Going against the norm 61
Afterword..69

Acknowledgements

From top left to bottom right: Abigail Oguntuyi, Ashaba Hiport, Charles Neser, Ettuon Slabbert, Kimberly Nacpil, Mikaela Gabriel, Nick Baird, Quratulain Aisha, Shrinkhal Shrestha, Zhansaya Bakirova

Additional Acknowledgments

Ali Usman, Allen Chang, Ilekhomon Odion, Lulu Amaniyah

An open wound

This week, I was interviewed by a journalist. During the interview I was reminded of time about 10 years ago when I was running one of my earlier businesses. Thinking about it, I realised that the topic discussed tapped upon one of the most difficult times in my entrepreneurial journey.

Going through the beginning of my business journey was hard, but nothing could prepare me for the experience of having a team of staff under my wing.

My first healthcare practice was growing, and I was extremely pleased that I was providing jobs for about 10 people through my business, but new times also brought new challenges.

As the number of employees increased, the mountains of HR paperwork followed. I was trying to juggle things when people were sick or on holidays, dealing with customer complaints, upset staff, talk behind my back. Eventually it got so bad for me, that it became one of the catalysts for selling the business. It took a period of time to recover mentally, and I told myself that I would never hire anyone ever again.

I learned lessons that I could never learn sitting through a seminar. It was tough, but I recovered, and you know what? I started hiring again a year later, but this time with clearer boundaries and better management. Even writing about it now brings me a few goosebumps!

The Voice of Small Business: Tough Times

In this book you will read about amazing stories of people learning their lessons and overcoming hardship. You will read about people who have had to recover from being homeless sitting on the roadside, people having to overcome difficulties to support their families, and even needing to eat their own business stock to survive another day. Some amazing recoveries from dire situations. Then you will also read about people needing to find customers, having their ideas laughed at, and having to learn from trial and error.

I interview 10 entrepreneurs around the world and ask them the following questions.

What was the toughest time in your business journey and what led up to this hardship?

How did you overcome this difficult time?

Did you change the way you conduct business after overcoming this tough time?

Can you provide a word of wisdom for an entrepreneur facing a tough time in business?

When you read these stories, take heart that hardships in business are experienced by every entrepreneur globally. Take encouragement from these people, learn from their lessons and enjoy!

From eviction to success

Ettuon Slabbert

At the age of 18 years old, I moved from my hometown to a city called Johannesburg where I started working in a crate manufacturing company. My family was a lot closer to me at the time and they invited me to a family get-together where I and my cousins started talking about potential business ideas. They mentioned that there was a huge gap in the petroleum sector where people with no financial backing could start a business as a middleman/broker. This would mean that you stand in the gap between end users, such as logistics companies, and suppliers, who have the diesel depot supplying the fuel.

I went home that evening and started to do some research on this and to my utter amazement, there was a gap that needed to be filled. The very next day after work, I went to my accountant to register a diesel distribution business. At this point in time, I needed to build a whole company from the ground up. I had no emails, websites, or even business cards. This created a huge problem as the existing businesses were well-established. I had to reach out to somebody that could help me kick-start this process. I started talking to my mother one evening and she suggested I reach out to my older brother because he was in digital marketing and website design.

When I was done with the conversation, I called my brother and explained to him my idea and what I needed to have in order to start trading as a business. My brother said he would help me get on my feet. He created a website for my business, emails, and business cards. I was delighted! I finally started seeing some progress and this inspired me to keep on pushing toward the goals I had set out.

What was the biggest hardship in your business and what led up to this hardship?

Everything that I needed was put in place to start but, there was an obstacle that I had to face. I still had a job at the crate manufacturing company that paid my bills and put a roof over my head. I couldn't just leave that for a shot in the dark. So, during my lunch breaks, I started to call fuel suppliers and inquired about pricing. The prices they gave me to start off with were not great but, I didn't know at the time that you needed to move large quantities of fuel to get better pricing.

That created a hurdle because I didn't have a client base to justify getting good prices. I had to think of an idea. I then decided to first call potential clients and ask them at what price point would they consider moving their business to me and what volumes/liters of fuel they were using for their truck. I roughly spoke to 250 companies and managed to get confirmations and potential purchase orders from about 22 of those. This meant that I had a possible 2,000,000 liters of diesel that would be purchased from me if I gave them the pricing they required.

I then went back to the fuel suppliers and said to them I have 2,000,000 liter diesel orders but I would require a certain price. After a few calls back and forth they gave in and gave me the price I asked for. I then went back to the same 22 clients and sent them quotations to get business from them. Unfortunately, 6 clients declined the offer but, on the other hand, 16 accepted and I officially had a business. There was still some lingering doubt in my mind because I just moved up to Johannesburg and I had made a commitment to work at the crate manufacturing company. "What should I do?", I asked myself. "Should I give up a set salary or should I take the jump and go into the lions' den of entrepreneurs?"

How did you overcome this difficult time?

I decided to leave my stable job at the age of 18 with no financial security and no certainty of where the next paycheck would come from. Not long after leaving my job, things started to get rough. I couldn't afford my rent, I couldn't afford to buy food, and the list goes on. I had too much pride to call my mother and my brother to tell them about the difficulty I was facing. Doubt started to set in because my client was not ordering as they promised.

The day finally arrived when I couldn't pay my rent and I was kicked out of my house. Out of the blue, I received a call from one of my friends that just wanted to check up on me. They saw I was stuck on the side of the road with nowhere to go. He immediately said to me, "take everything you own and move in with me until you are back on your feet."

The biggest fear I had to overcome was fighting self-doubt about my abilities in my business.

So the very next day, I woke up at my friend's house and I started to fight this mental blockage that I was facing. I made it my goal to call 50 potential clients a day and send quotations to all of those clients. I programmed my brain into believing that if only one of those clients a day said yes and started to place an order, I would have 30 new clients every month. So I called day in and day out until the results started speaking for themselves.

Did you change the way you conduct business after overcoming this tough time?

My goal from that point on was to continue with my dedication and keep with the discipline that I set to grow the business. Three months passed and the results were mind-blowing. I kept with the routine I set myself and day by day my client database grew. After 4 months of smart and hard work, I was able to move out and get my own house again. I learned that you need to have a structure in a business not only for the business itself, but also for yourself because at the end of the day if you decide to go into the world of entrepreneurs, you are the business.

Without you at the helm, there is no business. I learned that all the setbacks and hardships that one goes through are the lessons we learn from to build a successful business. Priority is a major part of your discipline in building the business. The late nights you used to spend partying turn into late nights working in front of your laptop getting stuff ready for the next day. Your whole mindset must change. You must embrace change and not always see hardship as a curse but more as a learning curve on how to build a better business.

Can you provide a word of wisdom for an entrepreneur facing a tough time in business?

A word of advice I can give to young entrepreneurs like myself would be to take risks but remember that success in your business will be the result of your preparation, working hard, and learning from your failures. Do not repeat your old bad habits. Instead, set good new habits that will prepare you to become a better version of yourself. Never give up. Every "no" a client gives you is one step closer to the "yes" that will change your destination for the business. That brings me on to hard and smart work.

Not every hard-working man is successful. Do your homework before starting a new venture "Smart work" works as hard as possible to see it through. Be persistent because some days you will feel like giving up but it's those days that make you stronger. It is those days that give you the edge on your competition and when you are blessed with a great positive cash flow business, be grateful and do not forget your roots. I do hope my story inspires a lot of you to get up and face those giants that are standing in front of you. Get the job done. You can do it!

The Voice of Small Business: Tough Times

Succeeding was a necessity

Abigail Oguntuyi

"The world is your oyster, they say; so I decided to own it." I am a 19 year old writer and online store business owner. I started my business on November 29th, 2021 when I was broke and in desperate need of money. Growing up, the business world had always piqued my interest. I don't know if my love for it started from the cool cash,I saw people counting or the accomplishment that came with owning something you could boldly call your own. Either way, I loved it and I wanted it.

Growing up in a family of five, it was a hard struggle for us as my mother was the only one working to support my sisters and me. You can just imagine the weight on her shoulders which considerably increased as we entered higher education institutions. I've always been a child who dreamt of the bigger picture and wanted something grand, glamorous even, but that dream was thrown in a bin when poverty struck its evil sword at my barely beating heart. I was in school, and my mother was barely managing while trying to find a balance of her own after a messy separation from my father. I didn't have money and I needed to get my hand on it legally and pridefully I suppose.

It was then that the idea of my business came to mind. Fashion has always come easy to me and I wanted something in my element with the excuse that if at all I can't start as grand as I wanted, I could at least make it about something I'm passionate about. That, ladies and gentlemen, was how I started "Nonpareil Accessories".

What was the toughest time in your business journey and what led up to this hardship?

"My biggest hardship in my business was what led me to my business." I think by now, we can all guess what that problem was. Money. We define money as a current medium of exchange and anyone who has money – loads of it – has power. Money, at that time to me, meant survival. It was the answer to my prayers, and it still is. I lacked capital. Capital is what every business owner needs to take that bold step. I had a lot to buy before starting my own business. I needed to buy my products in bulk, find a small space to display those products like a shop, get branded shopping polythene bags, pay for a customized business logo and advertisements, and much more, but I couldn't afford all that.

I wanted to take a loan at that time, but I thought myself too young coupled with the uncertainty that clouded my mind due to the fear of every business owner newbie, "what if my business fails?" I was too broke to take a loan and I didn't even want to risk it as I was scared that things might not go my way. If there was one thing, I feared the most then, it was the outcome of my decision. That, I had no answer to at that time. It was a huge step for me which made me decide that if my business did not succeed,

I didn't want to drag others down with me nor did I want to drown myself in loans. I wouldn't survive it. I wanted to inform my mum and sisters but like I said, I didn't want to drag others with me. I just couldn't add more to my mum's plate and my sisters were striving hard to keep the family afloat. It wasn't what they needed at the time. Besides, my feeble heart then searched for any word of discouragement that would put an end to my madness. Or so I thought. I badly wanted to start just as badly as I wanted to stop. It was an endless battle within me but my unrelenting, goal achieving, and risk-taking spirit told me to go on, for my solution was within my arms reach.

How did you overcome this difficult time?

"The bigger your walls; the harder they fall. Make sure to knock 'em good." Truly they say that you can do anything with the internet and since then I've promised myself if I'm to cross paths with the generations of the men who came up with this great invention, I'd give them a big kiss. Thank you so much Vinton and Bob. I was desperate, very desperate and so I went to the first thing that I usually run to to solve my mysteries – the internet.

I googled "how to start a business without capital" and that was where I got my idea from. I decided to make my business an online store as I had neither the money to buy my own space nor the funds to buy products in bulk. I knew what I wanted but I just couldn't afford it. It was then I found a popular online retail service based in China. It's focused on selling various products from household tools to skin care, fashion, electronics, etc. This platform allows sellers to sell their durable products to customers all over the world at an affordable price. It was then that I got my idea. I thought to myself "Since you have no money to buy in bulk or own a space, why not make your business an online store based on preorder?"

Believe me when I say it was the most brilliant idea ever! Pre Order goods/products are those that are only available based on customers' requests and it might take a while for the customers to get their products as they are usually shipped. I obviously didn't just jump into that glorious opportunity without testing it first, so I decided to order a necklace from them. A very affordable necklace was delivered 4 weeks after payment in good condition and quality. I knew then that this was the little push I was looking for.

The name of the store was certain, the products and space issue was solved. All that was left was my business logo and getting customers. I couldn't afford a graphic designer, so I went on online, played with a few designs and BAM! My very own business logo. This made me realize that one doesn't always have to start big for a business, after all, Rome wasn't built in a day. All that matters is that you take those steps and put in your hard work and also pray it works.

I needed customers. I paid an old friend of mine who happened to be an upcoming influencer a stipend to help me promote my new business. I wasn't expecting a large crowd and at the same time I wasn't expecting two customers that night. Two customers turned into ten customers in a week. I was elated.

Did you change the way you conduct business after overcoming this tough time?

"Now, those walls are down but my pride isn't." I've experienced what it's like to be a customer and I'm still experiencing it. I've gone through bad customer service that left me pissed and promising to never come back. I've also gone through the professional ones that left me in awe at how one can be so diligent, competent and responsible. I remember my birthday last year when I ordered a dress that was a little overpriced but it was beautiful, so I put up with it but the customer service… It was horrible!

I ordered my dress three weeks before my birthday to avoid unnecessary stress, but I got it a day after my birthday all thanks to the multiple angry messages I sent and calls I made to the vendor. I remember having a headache for days. From that day on, I swore to myself that if I ever owned a business, I'd treat my customers fairly and charge them fairly. I'll make sure they get the best treatment which would leave them coming back to get more – if only I knew I would be starting my own business a few months from then. I can't say I fully understand humans, but I do know one thing that humans rely on and that's trust. No matter how big your business is or how large or small your customers are; let them be reassured that they can always count on you. Let them know you have their best interest at heart. Don't be selfish or greedy. Don't overcharge them because you never know how many customers are lining up behind that one customer.

I was using a foreign platform which was something that totally slipped my mind when I first started price tagging my products online. It was after my first three customers that I realized all I made in total from them was a very small amount. It wasn't profitable to me at all, coupled with the transport fee I'd spent going to take the products from the local post office, which is where all my products ended up. So, I had to calculate approximately the amount my bank charged, then I added that to the price of the main product and I ensured that I had a better profit from each sale.

The price changing process was actually smooth for me as within a short period of time, I'd created a professional yet trusting relationship with my customers. After a little explanation about why the prices were increased, they went along with it.

At that moment, business was going well. I wasn't rich but at least I didn't feel poor anymore.

Can you provide a word of wisdom for an entrepreneur facing a tough time in business?

Don't give up! Don't you ever! If there's one thing you should keep trying in life, it is getting up again when life knocks you down. Life isn't a bed of roses. It's not sweet for all of us. A man once said that you can kill a dream but you can't kill hope. Or maybe you can't kill a dream after all since hope is what births dreams. Never lose hope. I didn't lose hope, in fact, I had no choice to lose hope as it was the only thing keeping me in that line of business. It was hope that saved me and it can save you too.

Maybe things are not going as planned for you. Maybe customers are not rushing in like they should or used to. Maybe you are not making as much profits as before. Maybe you are about to lose your business to a loan shark…maybe. Have you tried another method? Have you walked another path? If the road is rough, why not pass through the grassland or level the ground by filling the holes. There's always another way, never forget that. Think outside the box. You can do it! I did it! My business isn't perfect either. My business started running slow a while ago but I decided to do something different and it's picking up again.

Do you think there'll be any solution to any of the problems in the world if we all gave up? No! There wouldn't. Some people tried so many times to make something of themselves so what makes you different. What's stopping you?

Start by being positive today, prophecy it every day and one day it will manifest.

The Voice of Small Business: Tough Times

A risk that paid off

Nick Baird

I'm a 29 year old MA student studying public policy. My career path has meandered since finishing my bachelor's in 2016 but the longest standing professional work I've done is running Nick of Time Textbooks. Since starting I've sold $500,000 worth of books on Amazon.

My start with the business began a bit before 2016. A family friend showed me his side hustle in Las Vegas where he bought all kinds of stuff from garage sales and estate sales for resale on online platforms. His closet looked like it was being shared by a 7 year old collecting building bricks, an adult who really liked collectible board games, and a woman with a refined sense of clothing style. It was odd but apparently lucrative for him. I decided to give it a shot.

After he showed me the ropes, I got to work going to garage sales during the midwestern summer. My first few outings, I spent maybe $150 on what amounted to junk. Turns out old cartoon coffee mugs aren't collectible after all! I persisted though. After a while, I discovered that focusing on a niche was the way to go. Why spend hours looking up the value of a lawnmower, printing press, and collectible comic only to discover I can't haggle the price low enough to make a profit when I can scan a book, know its value in 30 seconds, and offer the owner a dollar for it? The decision was easy.

From here I discovered a honey pot at my local university where I could buy used textbooks from students. Now I had a source of inventory that would come to me; this is how I've paid the rent for the last six years.

What was the toughest time in your business journey and what led up to this hardship?

There were two things that were difficult. When I first took the plunge from sourcing a few books at a time from garage sales to buying hundreds at a time from students, I had to have ten to twenty thousand dollars to spend in a two week period of time. That was a lot of money for a fresh college graduate to come up with. Not only that, but the first time I purchased such a large amount of inventory I was absolutely losing my mind from the nerves. What if they don't sell? Can I still afford to pay rent? Will I have to move back in with my parents? These were the things on my mind for about a month between December and January 2016.

The second problem was marketing. I'd figured out how to sell everything I could buy, and how to pay for whatever inventory was available, but learning to grow the business proved difficult. Between building email lists, handwriting letters, a website, social media ads, and physical signage spread around campus, I've tried quite a few things over the years to get more attention. I couldn't say how much I've spent on this over the years but by most business standards it hasn't been much.

How did you overcome this difficult time?

It took a few months to scramble the money together for the first time but between a small bank loan (cosigned by family) and loans from both grandparents and my father, I was able to come up with a bankroll large enough to purchase all the books available to me. As for dealing with the fear there was really nothing for it but to be patient and keep faith. Luckily, it all went well, and I never had to explain to my family members why I would need more time to pay back the loans they gave me.

Marketing has actually proven so difficult that my yearly sales have been basically the same since I started; 25k in winter and 50k in summer. I've tried half a dozen things but none of them stuck. Marketing isn't my strength it seems. I built a website but didn't know how to drive traffic to it. I had gotten lucky with one university but couldn't figure out how to spread to another. My social media ads didn't convert and cost more money than the sales on the other end were worth. There's lots of competition online in this space.

Did you change the way you conduct business after overcoming this tough time?

My overcoming this hardship was more stoic acceptance and gratitude than a rags to riches "I 10x'd my business in five years" story. I'd say I'm disappointed but I'm really not. The business provided exactly as much money as I needed to squeak by as a recent college graduate working only three months out of the year. As a result, I was able to experiment with half a dozen other career paths without regard for how well they paid. I've taken unpaid internships on political campaigns, done volunteer work for online communities, an unpaid internship at a think tank, spent time as a licensed financial advisor, and now I'm back in school for my MA in public policy. I won't make much when I graduate, it's what I get for going into the helping professions, but I'll be able to sleep at night and feel energized during the day working on something I care about.

I've been a bit more efficient with the inventory I do manage to buy. In the early days, I sold lower than I could have because I was afraid it wouldn't sell at all. Now I have diamond hands and can wait until the last minute to get the absolute highest selling price I can.

Can you provide a word of wisdom for an entrepreneur facing a tough time in business?

I'm no wise monk but I can give it a shot. Do the mental preparation you need in order to come to terms with the risk you need to take in order to face your business hardship. Mine was the first time I spent $10,000 on buying books without being certain things would sell. I did the mental calculus and decided that I could always fall back on my parents and that in the grand scheme of things $10,000 really wasn't that much. I had more in undergraduate student loans after all!

Another piece of advice I would have for you is to keep in mind why you're in business. There are plenty of reasons, but I think it's wrong to be in business purely for money. Obviously, that's a big piece but, in my eyes, the reason to run your own business is so that your success is rewarded by buying you *time*. It's the most valuable resource we get in this life and when we can transition into a world where we're not attached to a 9-5 year round, we get to experience the joys of life that maybe don't pay us money but do bring us fulfillment.

The Voice of Small Business: Tough Times

The success of a warm heart

Kimberly Nacpil

I am one of the owners of a family business, a small lending company here in the Philippines, a corporation engaged in granting loans from its own capital funds. Basically, we are offering loans to small and micro businesses for the purpose of obtaining additional capital for their business. They can use the loan to expand their business or for additional stocks.

We currently have around one thousand accounts with loans ranging from three thousand pesos (50 USD) to fifty thousand pesos (850 USD) for a short-term loan. This business only started as a personal lending with a starting capital of fifty thousand pesos (850 USD), lending to neighbors and friends' way back in 2016 with not more than fifteen creditors. However, since money is the easiest product that you can sell, it makes our business grow rapidly such that in just three years, we were able to cater to around five thousand creditors with five branches, managing more than fifty employees.

I personally didn't imagine that we would be able to grow like this as it happened so fast. Honestly, this is not the industry that I studied in college as I took my bachelor's degree in Tourism Management, but since it's a family business, I have no choice but to help our family in taking over some of the main roles in running the business. I was assigned the Human

Resources and Payroll Manager where I processed recruitments and payroll of our staff.

What was the toughest time in your business journey and what led up to this hardship?

There are lots of hardships in starting, running, and rebuilding in this business. First, the hardship in starting this business was the transition from being a warmhearted to coldhearted person.

Second, in order to manage the clients, we need to use all of the possible ways just to make sure that the client will be able to pay us back their loans. We use a lot of different ways that sometimes require us to be coldhearted.

Third is the economy. We have been all affected by the recent lockdowns due to the COVID-19 pandemic where the government and private offices are all required to temporarily close, and in our country, we have been locked down for three months. That three month lockdown really affected us since our clients are all business persons and their businesses have been closed for more than three months. Some of them permanently closed their business resulting in them being unable to pay their outstanding balance to us. That lockdown caused us to permanently close four of our five branches and reduced our manpower due to high deficit on income and expenses. We even struggled to pay monthly bills and staff salaries, faced delayed payment penalties, and received warnings and payment demand letters. We had to make hard decisions like selling and putting our properties on mortgage such as cars and real estate properties just to cope up with the dues and to support the business.

Lastly, one of the biggest hardships was terminating staff due to company downsizing caused by the lack of company income. On one occasion, I personally served a retrenchment letter to one of our staff who was a pioneer to the company. She was with us the longest and her performance was outstanding, however; the branch that she was assigned was one of the branches that we decided to permanently close. We have no choice but to end her contract with us. Upon serving the letter, I learned that she was a single mother with two children and the only one in her family that provides their daily needs. Hearing her saying that hit us differently and at that time, I realized that we weren't the only ones who were struggling.

How did you overcome this difficult time?

Currently, we are moving forward from what happened to the company. We talked to our staff about the current situation and the crisis of the company. We told them about the problems that need urgent solutions, discussed all the possibilities we might face, and motivated each other to keep moving forward as there is no other option for us to survive but to keep moving forward. We have set aside our pride and humbly asked for their help to support us and work like they also owned the company. We became more open to the staff and discussed a lot of possible plans for each problem. We have learned to learn new and different approaches to every problem.

We also became more prepared and alert at all times, grabbing the most of every opportunity as it could arise when you least expect. Being equipped to seize an opportunity at all times really helps us to overcome our hardships.

Right now, we are glad that we are able to re-open our second branch again. We now have two fully operational and fully staffed branches. It's still far from our previous five branches, but what is important is that we are able to make progress after the downturn of our business. Progress is something to celebrate.

Did you change the way you conduct business after overcoming this tough time?

We had to make a series of changes to rebuild our business. From the first hour when I enter the office, I do things that I usually avoided such as having a coffee with the staff to start the day and considering their ideas in making decisions. Having done it now for five months, it changes everything. Solving problems became easier as we got a lot of ideas. I felt like I truly understood them now, making every interaction smooth and the workplace became light as we all began to feel like it is an extension of our home. We have realized that no one succeeds in business alone; rebuilding our business as a great team has surely bolstered the company to get back on the track.

We also changed our motivation in doing business. Unlike before when we were running the business for profit only, we are now in this business to give employment opportunities and to help our creditors to expand and build their businesses. Changing our motivation really changed everything and it was one of the best decisions we have made. It is like planting an apple seed and expecting an apple tree.

Currently, we are humbly expanding our connection in this line of industry. Attending different gatherings from businesses from the same industry, building connections and learning new things with them also saved us from our downturn.

Can you provide a word of wisdom for an entrepreneur facing a tough time in business?

Hardships and business are like pen and paper, they're inseparable. If you want to be successful, hardships must be accepted as a part of running a business. They will build and mold you to become successful.

Attitudes like bravery to take the risk and a strong positive mindset are the main keys in facing hardships in business. Maybe you have those personalities and are still struggling in business. Try to take a breath and accept the fact that no successful business is created easily without hardships. If you are facing hardship right now, consider that as a challenge to make you stronger and move you closer to success. Try different methods or solutions. You will never know the outcome of your effort unless you actually do it. Failure is much better than regret for not trying.

Grow your network. Learning and inspiration doesn't just come from inside you. One of the best ways to solve your hardships is to learn from other entrepreneurs at the same stage of business as you. Try to avoid competition and instead exchange your own knowledge for theirs. This will make networking mutually beneficial, perhaps leading to potential opportunities in the future.

Be humble and accept feedback. It can be tempting to act like you know everything and put on a front as a strong entrepreneurial character. However, you shouldn't always expect your ideas to become successes. Your role as the entrepreneur is to produce a lot of ideas to get the right one. Part of that process is successfully proving your ideas are no good and failure is part of making progress. Also, hearing honest feedback and acting on it is essential if you want your business to be successful. It can hurt your pride but sometimes criticism can be your best friend. Identifying the problems and acting on them will lead to further success and growth.

Lastly, learn to rest. Entrepreneurs have higher pressures than a lot of other job roles. It's important to schedule a rest or some ways you can disconnect from work like spending time with family or doing the things that you love. Although these activities might not seem important, it is vital to occupy your mind elsewhere to alleviate stress and it will make your mind more refreshed with ideas. Consider it as your reset button whenever you feel like you are running out of solutions.

Scaling the business to survive

Charles Neser

I am in my 20s with a Bachelors, Honors and masters in animal science. I lived my entire life in South Africa and, fortunately, the regulation on red meat is not as strict as in other countries. After noticing that more and more people were looking for a healthier alternative to traditional red meat products (beef and mutton), I saw a gap in the market. As venison (game) has much lower cholesterol content than other red meat products, it is widely accepted, however; the only problem is how people obtain the meat.

It was then that I started 'Doringdraad' – a venison (game) product business. We hunt the game and process the meat into desirable products such as droewors, biltong (a type of jerky), sausages and other products people desire. We even went a step further when the trend of people preferring to stay at home continued to rise. We decided that a free weekly delivery system should be implemented, delivering fresh products right to your doorstep. This gave us an edge on the butchery and, since our delivery was free and most traditional butcheries weren't, we were miles ahead of the competition. Sales were going great, we made $80,000 USD in our first 3 years, which is a lot considering currency conversion. The only thing that could stop us was our own ego…

The Voice of Small Business: Tough Times

What was the toughest time in your business journey and what led up to this hardship?

Our biggest problem was scalability without taking risks. So after 3 amazing years, COVID came, everything shut down, businesses closed and people stayed at home. However, people still needed to eat right? After 2 months of hard lockdown and a true test of patience we were back in business, sourcing our meat from farmers in close vicinity to our business operation.

Strict adherence to COVID regulations was practiced which, when working with stubborn farmers, was a challenge on its own. The business was now booming, we left the competition in the dust as most feedlots were still unable to operate. The butcheries did not have any meat to sell – that means more clients for us. We saw an influx of new orders, 357% to be precise. We were struggling to keep up, the demand outweighed the supply. We desperately needed to scale our business.

However, our business runs on a high liquidity basis, meaning the majority of our capital is put into work by purchasing stock. This means that we do not have a lot of capital left for other expenses – especially not expanding. We were in a tight spot: scale and risk losing everything or stay stagnant and risk losing clients due to not having products or decreased quality of products due to high output.

How did you overcome this difficult time?

After numerous meetings and rigorous brainstorming sessions, we came to the simple conclusion: Nothing ventured, nothing gained. Failure to take the risk is a risk itself. Let me explain. Our competition was quickly catching on. We were already losing clients to people with inferior quality products to ours (tested and reviewed) due to the simple fact that we didn't have products to sell. Sure, our loyal clients stayed but our loyal clients have been with us for more than 3 years. We had the majority stake in the local market. We wouldn't let it go that easily. Fortunately, we had built up some assets during this time and interest rates were still low.

So, we took a loan against our assets utilizing the low interest rates. Our plan was to pay off the loan as quickly as possible as, with my economics background, I knew that interest rates were not going to stay low for long. So, instead of risking the majority of our capital to expand, we simply allocated the profit from a set amount of weekly sales to go toward paying off the loan. This meant that yes, we did not have as much liquidity as we'd had hoped for to operate comfortably, but we were not pushing ourselves into danger zones.

We successfully scaled our business by purchasing new and bigger equipment, a larger processing facility and onboarding more staff. We were able to increase production by 150% ensuring supply equaled demand. Now you might think, "Well, the butcheries probably opened up again and demand would've fallen for our products". Truth be told, the clients enjoyed our products so much that they switched loyalty. Just goes to show that if you have a product of excellent quality and there is an opportunity in the market, you should do everything in your power to take advantage of that without compromising your integrity.

Did you change the way you conduct business after overcoming this tough time?

We changed our entire point of view towards risk. We realized that calculated risk is not really risk at all, if managed properly. Yes, our plan could have backfired, and demand could have dropped, but if you believe in your product and you have done your research you can rest assured. The numbers don't lie! If demand were supposed to suddenly drop, we would simply sell the newly purchased equipment and lease out the new facility to someone else. We would break even from our loan, not even losing money.

There is a saying, 'Failure to plan is planning to fail'. My entire business fundamentally revolves around this statement now. I now set out target goals for our business: weekly, monthly, quarterly and yearly. They are almost impossible to achieve, but because extra bonuses get paid out if targets are achieved, it motivates the employees to put in the extra effort. Even that was a calculated risk! The increase in efficiency worked by the employees offsets the bonus' cost. Thus, I've learned risk and planning go hand in hand. A combination of both can be to the greatest of your advantage, but the former lacking the latter is a recipe for disaster! I will never do business again without first having a plan because a risky plan is still a plan.

Can you provide a word of wisdom for an entrepreneur facing a tough time in business?

Stick to your values. Do not compromise your or your business' integrity for the sake of making a quick buck or saving the company from bankruptcy. When everything comes crashing down, the final thing that will last is your name and reputation. It is irreplaceable. Once lost or ruined it takes years to build up that consumer trust again.

Treat every customer as if they were your best paying customer. This sows a great consumer confidence in a business. Every client wants to feel important. It unlocks value in the form of loyalty which in turn converts to reliability. Reliability in knowing you will have a set amount of sales every week and reliability in knowing that you will have a free marketing medium. Word-of-mouth advertising is the most effective advertising there is – PROVEN.

Patience is my final piece of advice - if you do the steps mentioned above when facing hardship and you do them long enough to ensure that the business survives, if enough time has passed the business will not only survive but will begin to thrive. I have a huge amount of respect for anyone who pursues the path less traveled relating to entrepreneurship, and to finish off I'd like to say keep working and putting in the effort. The day will come when all of the late nights and early mornings are worth it!

The Voice of Small Business: Tough Times

Trial and error is a great teacher

Mikaela Gabriel

I started my small online business at the age of 18. I studied in an Aviation School which gave me the idea to sell aircraft-related items that are affordable to students.

I started with a $1 capital, and I was able to buy 5 aircraft keychains which I sold for $0.50 a piece. From there, I went on to buy more after I got back the capital and the profit. From exclusively selling keychains, I have expanded my products to other accessories such as necklaces and bracelets that also have airplane pendants.

A couple of years later, I graduated and lost my market. I changed my products to personalized souvenirs where I hand stamped every letter. I launched it just in time for the Christmas season, hence the success, and I sold 2000 + items in 2 months, however, it was draining and exhausted me.

Then I thought I should try selling ready-made products instead – maybe it would be less exhausting. Knowing that Filipinos love traveling and dressing up, I switched to selling winter coats. Unlike my previous products which are small and can be kept in a small cabinet, these coats were bulky and took up a lot of space. I had to sell them quickly right before the pandemic started. I once again knew it wasn't the right product.

I was able to save up and tried another line in semi-formal women's clothing. I've been running this for 2.5 years now and I have earned six figures in Philippine Peso annually. It's something that I really enjoy, and I have expanded my market to those that are working or just really want to dress nicely.

What was the toughest time in your business journey and what led up to this hardship?

The biggest hardship that I've faced is finding the right product. You need to allot so much of your time studying the market, your competitors, which platforms you are going to use, pricing, how you would sell the product, what strategies are you going to apply, and most importantly, you need to gauge if it's something that really interests you and can see yourself doing for a long time. It's difficult to be consistent in a business if you do not enjoy what you are doing or if you're not talking to the right audience, or if you simply don't know how to sell your product.

Many factors led up to this hardship such as a lack of budget to do what you envision; it could also be that you are not in the right state to brainstorm and conceptualize and don't have an idea of where to find suppliers etc. Competitors are also something to consider, especially now that almost everything can be bought online. Direct suppliers are taking over the internet. You must find a way to make your product/service stand out from the rest, hence a lot of people are doing customization and adding a little bit of their own twist to products.

How did you overcome this difficult time?

I have overcome this hardship by letting myself fail and learn. I'm lucky to have started my startup at a young age, which means that I have had plenty of time to get up, start again, and learn from my mistakes. I have tried selling various products and it has been difficult for me to stay consistent. It seemed like I was losing interest after a certain period of time even if I was trying to enjoy the process of learning.

It took me 4 years of trial and error before finding the product that I loved and could see myself being invested in for a long time. It didn't really come easy and it's something that can't be fixed overnight. I needed to truly evaluate myself whether my startup was worth all the time and effort that I put into it. I needed to list my negotiables and non-negotiables, how is this going to benefit the customers, is it good for the environment. I needed to focus on my vision and be realistic to myself on how I see my product stand in the market for years.

With the trends changing and technology evolving quickly, these steps were the ones that have effectively helped me get back into the game.

Did you change the way you conduct business after overcoming this tough time?

How I run my business after overcoming the hardship of finding the right product changed tremendously. I was putting a lot of pressure on myself with the previous products that I sold because they say, there is likely something wrong if you never go out of stock. I remember a saying from my supply chain management class; "A full warehouse is a bad warehouse" because the purpose of a warehouse is to store and move products, and although I do not have a warehouse, the same concept applies — if my products are staying on the shelf for a long time, something is likely not right and that I must do something about it.

The product that I'm selling now is, so far, the only one that has kept me excited for years. It is something that makes me want to talk to the customers, answer all their queries enthusiastically, and exert efforts on marketing materials and photography. It's something that I value, something that I don't allow to be bargained at their lowest. I chose products that are not perishable, and those that are easy to store – and most importantly, something that I see a potential of selling for more years to come.

Can you provide a word of wisdom for an entrepreneur facing a tough time in business?

If you're a young adult trying to explore the business world, go forth and do your trial and error. Your 20s are the best time to make mistakes and learn. And if you're above the 20s, still do not get pressured. It is never too late to start exploring and you'll never know the outcome unless you try. Know that it isn't going to be easy.

There will be a lot of breakdowns, a lot of times where you feel like you're not selling enough, and a lot of times questioning yourself whether there is something wrong with what you are doing. Do not get discouraged if you feel like you don't have enough capital. There are a lot of ways to start small and build until you achieve your vision.

Do not feel guilty for resting. Take all the time you need to pause and reflect if you feel like things aren't going as you planned and thought they would be. You should always expect that there will be unforeseen challenges, and you should always be ready to face them. Do not stop trying. Know the worth of the service you provide, and do not stop until your goal is reached.

The Voice of Small Business: Tough Times

On the brink of failure

Ashaba Hiport

I am a masters degree holder in Management Science and Engineering, degree in Project Planning and Entrepreneurship. I do Cuniculture farming for meat and wool. I'm also an experienced researcher and a business mentor and I'm excited to share my story.

My journey into Cuniculture farming started in May 2020, a few months after the outbreak of the covid-19 pandemic. Early in 2020, the World Health Organization declared covid-19 a public health emergency of international concern and that is when my life started changing. I had a job at an oil company. at an entry level, but the pay was good enough to cover my rent, transport expenses, food, and a small balance for saving.

Upon the covid-19 announcement, our CEO called for a meeting and briefed us about the pandemic. He suggested to management that we start working in shifts to reduce congestion and contact at work. As cases increased and panic mounted, the government announced a partial lockdown. During this time public transport was closed and businesses were disrupted, and this prompted the company to downsize. Unfortunately, I was among those who were laid-off. Everything was happening so fast that our organization had no plan for severance or unemployment benefits or any other form of compensation.

In March 2022, I was just home, sustaining myself on the money I had saved. Toward the end of March 2022, I had to pay rent for April and my account balance came down even more. It was at this point that I began to imagine what life would be like if I continued eating without earning, if I was going to manage rent and utilities bills. Trying to look for solutions, I thought of doing a business that would require small starting capital with quick returns on investment. I googled and read an article, "Rabbit farming in Kenya".

I was immediately inspired and motivated by the benefits of rabbit meat, growing demand for rabbit meat, the gestation period and the time they take to mature. Although the budget was more than my savings, I decided to look into some of the already existing factors that I could use to my advantage. I also wrote a business plan that I presented to my father for extra support. I had to move from Kampala to my village in Ibanda which, about 305 km away, where I could use family land without paying rent.

What was the toughest time in your business journey and what led up to this hardship?

The biggest hardship in my business was finding a market for rabbits and rabbit meat. In Uganda, rabbit meat retails on average $4.72 per kilogram and a mature rabbit costs $10.49 to $26.23 depending on the breed. Considering the above figures, it is clear that Cuniculture farming is very rewarding. The biggest challenge here was how to connect to that person or that buyer. There was a big disconnect between my rabbit farm and customers/consumers.

As a starter, I did not have enough money to buy a license from the Uganda Bureau of Standards and the necessary certificates to allow me to retail the meat in supermarkets and butcheries. I needed to find ways of connecting with customers.

One way I could have done this was to do contract farming. I reached out to my friend in Sheema District who was also rearing rabbits and he gave me a brilliant idea to join popular messaging groups for rabbit farmers, which I did. A few days later, I saw a post looking for someone who could supply 40 kg of rabbit meat on a weekly basis. I called and asked for details, and I was told I must sign a one year contract to supply meat. This also made the situation worse because the terms of the contract were so hard for me to meet.

Despite allowing my farm to grow to about 400 mature rabbits each with an average weight of 2.5 kgs (dead weight), I did not have the capacity to supply 40 kg per week for 12 months. It turned out that the only option I had to connect with customers was also challenging because of the unfavorable terms of the contract.

In the meantime, rabbits were giving birth and getting crowded, the structures demanded expansion, and the cost of feeding and treatment were also increasing. The business that I thought would be self-sustainable at that stage still needed money injected from the side. It even got to a point where I acquired a friendly loan to sustain the farm while I looked for a market.

How did you overcome this difficult time?

Overcoming the hardships took some time and before things got better, they had to get worse first. Before that, I was very conscious not to lose what I had already achieved. Since the business had no capacity to acquire a business loan, I got a friendly loan from a family member to take care of the expansion of structures, feeds and veterinary services as I continued looking for favorable contracts.

Knowing how delicate rabbits are, I did not want to compromise on feeds, veterinary services or allowing them to get crowded. If I did, this could have exposed rabbits to the risk of getting sick and ultimately incurring high costs on treatment or losing them. I decided to exercise some patience as I tried with other companies. Unfortunately, there was no success. Some companies wanted minimum supplies of 300 kg per month while others wanted rabbits with a minimum dead weight of 5 kg which I didn't have.

Out of frustration, I started slaughtering the rabbits that were meant for business for my own consumption. I sold some live ones to neighbors but only a few could afford to pay for a rabbit. I had to make it cheaper just to recover some money and phase out the business. On the other hand, society and culture also made it hard for me to sell rabbit meat. Most people in western Uganda do not like rabbit meat because of their resemblance to cats. So if I was to make good sales, I needed to look at other regions like central and eastern Uganda.

While I was slowly giving up, I didn't know I had inspired some members in my village. Some had even bought starting stock from my farm and had started their farms. I started getting strange calls, people asking me how I manage my rabbits, where I buy food for my rabbits, where I get market for my rabbit meat. Since I had read so much about rabbits and interacted with some potential buyers, to me this was an eye opener. I realized actually I don't have to be a rabbit farmer to do business. The industry had so many gaps that I could take advantage of. The questions that I was receiving from people made me realize the untapped opportunities and it was at that moment I decided to redefine my business model.

Did you change the way you conduct business after overcoming this tough time?

Ultimately, I ended up redefining my business model. I talked to my cousin who was into community-based programs and she advised me to join youth groups. When I joined youth groups, I introduced rabbit farming to them. At first they were hesitant, but later some members agreed to join. Even for the youth groups, their biggest question was, "where to get the market for rabbit meat". From my experience, I knew where the market was and I also knew what it takes to connect with the market and that is how I became a middle man and started using growers.

I could buy the rabbits from the organized groups at a reduced price, add a small margin for profits and sell in larger quantities. As long as I assured them about the market, they were willing to sell to me at a reduced price. The only challenge I had at this time was how to mobilize enough groups for a stable supply of meat. However, it was only a matter of time before more and more people joined and it became easy to mobilize and get the numbers I needed to sign bigger contracts.

This also opened new avenues for doing business. While my main focus was on creating markets, I also started supplying inputs such as feed, medicine, breeding boxes, feeders and much more. In Uganda, it's very hard to find experts in Cuniculture farming, but because I had read and experienced so much about rabbits, I was able to start sharing my knowledge and experiences at a small fee which earned me extra income. Since I already had structures in place, I decided to create a small model farm, where people could come pay a small fee and learn about Cuniculture farming.

From that day, I put my efforts into supporting youth and rabbit farmer groups. To ensure proper planning and sustainability of this business, farmer groups signed contracts and all members were to abide by the terms in the contracts.

Can you provide a word of wisdom for an entrepreneur facing a tough time in business?

Every stage in the cycle of business is not a straight line. You will meet hardships while starting a business, you will meet hardships while developing your business, you will meet hardships even after the business is mature, and you will certainly meet hardships even trying to close your business. Every stage along the value chain has its own challenges.

When you want to place your business at both ends of the value chain, you need to think about these challenges in a broad perspective. With a wider view of the challenges, you are able to decide whether you have or don't have the capacity to do the business. In case you don't have the capacity, it is not your fault and you should not give up on your dreams. The good news is, you can always find a starting point at any of the stages along the value chain, and the level of success will depend on your ability to overcome challenges at that particular stage. It will be that success that will inform your next strategic decision on growing your business.

As a starter I faced challenges and I know there are many more people out there who have faced similar challenges or are still facing them. There is a saying that goes, "a hen only picks what it can swallow". Personally, I did not think about that saying. I wanted to do everything, and the results were not good until I changed the way of doing my business as a middleman and worked backwards. I fully understand that every effort I made from the beginning matters, but I believe I could have done better if I chose to pick what I could swallow from the start.

Finally, I want to point out that the start is never easy and being a startup does not necessarily mean you must be at the beginning of the value chain. You can start from anywhere along the value and work towards any direction of your choice.

The Voice of Small Business: Tough Times

Maths is all part of business

Zhansaya Bakirova

I am a fast-food entrepreneur. It all started from the family who always praised my cooking talent. Everybody told me that only I can convert something as simple as bread into a piece of art and I told myself that this seems to be my best business opportunity. I always believed that the best work is the work that I enjoy because if I really enjoy my work, the outcome will always be unique and my clients will feel it, appreciate it, and understand that what I provide them is simply indispensable.

I didn't jump to opening a restaurant right away. I had to take it step by step because business is more than just a good product. I needed to have a cost-effective team that knew food delivery, taxes, legal documents etc. Also, I needed to have a budget that covered all details and aspects of the business.

I had to start with a home-based business in order to avoid the need to locate a huge sum of money for a startup, so I started making fast food and baked goods at home, and when I say fast food, I'm not talking about the cheeseburgers you can find everywhere. I am talking about unique recipes like Korean crunchy nuggets, Turkish Buns Achma and other recipes that you cannot just find in the shop next door.

In less than two years, I had my own loyal clients who wouldn't leave me for heaven. Finally, I could convert my home based business into a small restaurant, thanks to the loyal clients that guaranteed a continuous income for any business.

What was the toughest time in your business journey and what led up to this hardship?

I know how hard it is to convert an idea or a talent to a real business with tax ID, physical address, brand name, and a dedicated team of hard workers, but the hardest part of business is to locate enough funds. In order to determine how much money I needed, I had to make a list of all the items that I had to buy including new cookware. Such items must be rugged and require minimum maintenance over time. Also, I had to calculate the running cost including energy, like natural gas and electricity, cleaning resources including water and detergents. I also had to consider ads among the most critical running costs.

During the preliminary business calculations, I had to use an independent delivery service and I had to add the cost per delivery to each receipt individually based on its distance from my home. After all those calculations, I had to locate the required funds, so I bought most of the new rugged cookware using my savings. However, I had to raise most of my funds through close family and friends to avoid interest rates that would be added if I raised funds from sources outside the circles of family and friends.

The Voice of Small Business: Tough Times

How did you overcome this difficult time?

My strategy was to start from a home-based business and grow gradually. The good thing about gradual growth is that I never had to deal with a big problem. I actually dealt with problems in their simplest tiny forms and as my business grew, my problems grew with it, but this gradual growth was easily manageable compared to dealing with problems in their mature form all of a sudden.

Even though I started my business from home, I still had to spend lots of money because the cookware originally purchased to serve a family wasn't rugged or efficient enough compared to the ovens required to serve a business.

I had to make deliveries only within the nearby areas and add the cost of delivery to each order. Although this created some price differences for the same food items, I avoided hiring a full-time delivery biker and purchasing a bike!

I used ready-made plastic boxes to avoid paying for a big order of custom plastic box and I designed the brand name, logo box and stickers myself. I printed them using a cheap printing service and all of this didn't require any more than some average computer skills everybody has nowadays.

Finally, I minimized the marketing cost per client. For example, I started my marketing model by enlisting my restaurant in food directories and of course all orders had to be "take-away" since there is no space at home to receive clients.

Did you change the way you conduct business after overcoming this tough time?

Flexibility is considered the spirit of each and every startup. Edison failed 10,000 times before finding the right metal for his first light bulb and a recent space project was 6 years behind schedule before the first satellite made it into orbit. Always remember that failure is just another chance to learn a new thing.

I remember those first days after I launched my business and spent every single penny in my pocket making ads and spreading flyers here and there. After spending hours and days of hard work, nothing happened. NASA didn't order my amazing recipes for their astronauts before spending months in space and even the security guy of my own building didn't knock on my door.

Of course, I was depressed at the beginning, but gradually I understood that this is totally normal because there is always a waiting time between the moment your ad campaign starts, and when your ad campaign gets enough muscles to rotate the wheel of fortune.

In the case of restaurant business, the waiting time is typically just a couple of hours or even days, but in some businesses this waiting time can be weeks or months or even years. I realized that it is very important to choose the marketing campaign that stays active while waiting for clients to come. I kept in mind that the marketing campaign running cost is something critical for a startup, so all I had to do was adjust that cost to comply with the expected waiting time before the money machine started to work.

Can you provide a word of wisdom for an entrepreneur facing a tough time in business?

From my point of view, the most critical and overlooked part of a business is defining the niche of clients and defining cost effective ads to reach them. That's because any consumer compromises between his need for a certain product, the price of the product and the frequency of purchasing the product.

Not only that, but also one needs to put into consideration the competitors nearby, especially those that target the same niche of consumers. Some clients have loyalty to your competitors and those clients will not only ignore your product, but also, they won't even give you a chance to hand over your flier.

Finally, you need to minimize the marketing cost per client. This is a critical running cost overlooked by many startups. If you choose flyers, you need to know how many flyers you need to distribute to attract a new customer and, of course, you need to multiply the number of flyers by the cost per flier to obtain the cost of acquiring a new customer. Keep in mind, each niche of clients has a corresponding marketing means that attracts them and also marketing means that will repel them. Nobody markets cheap products using flyers simply because the cost of flyers will add to the cost of items resulting in a very expensive price, causing the fliers to repel customers instead of attracting them.

The Voice of Small Business: Tough Times

Failure as a badge of honor

Shrinkhal Shrestha

I am 27, from Nepal and I am running my research consulting firm, Kalithia Investment and Research. I specialize in preparing market research reports and business writing. I am currently doing my MBA in Business Analytics and completed my Bachelor's in Economics. I started my own company back in 2018 with my business partner. At first, we started the company to capitalize on the funding gaps in Nepal, as access to capital for newly established firms is challenging.

Similarly, we had also made plans to start our app, which focused on simulating the national stock exchange to educate new users and provide quality information. However, after hitting a few snags, we decided to take up a few research projects brought to us through our networks. We were doing well for the first year but as a long-term project collapsed, so did all our revenue streams since we depended on that company. Although we worked with a few big companies in Nepal to complete a market research report for them, we could not generate enough revenue for the work we had done.

Then, within a few months, we ran out of funds to keep the company running, and that is when we decided to forfeit taking a monthly salary from the company. After a few months, this practice needed to become more sustainable. My business partner received a golden opportunity to work at a reputed publicly listed bank. Eventually, I also decided to join a start-up e-commerce platform as a Digital Media Associate and left our company inactive.

What was the toughest time in your business journey and what led up to this hardship?

When starting my business, the most significant hardship I faced was a lack of reliable, professional legal and tax consultants. Coming from a developing country like Nepal, where government policies are not business-friendly, many business laws are not easily accessible to company owners. Similarly, there is rampant corruption; every company-related legal process has to go through a business lawyer or a registered auditor. This practice increases the cost to a company, and as business owners, we become intertwined in all the laws and do not know which rules are relevant.

I hired a legal and tax consultant, a dear friend of mine, but he failed to fulfill his duties to advise me on the most relevant laws. Although I hired him as a consultant, he was not accountable and did not take responsibility for recommending or informing me of business laws. In one instance, he failed to remind me to file my monthly VAT (Value-Added Tax) three months in a row and maintain a physical record. Even though the fine was little (around $35 per month), it looked terrible on my tax return filings. Therefore, the most significant hardship I faced was a lack of transparent business law. Secondly, I needed a reliable and accountable legal and tax consultant which was not readily available in Nepal.

How did you overcome this difficult time?

In a country like Nepal, we tend to hide our shortcomings and challenges. Nepalese society tends to look down on people who have failed. I felt like expressing my failures would humiliate me. However, I started to meet new people and as a form of small talk, we would exchange the challenges we would face, and I soon realized that I had not failed. It was a stepping stone and a minor pebble in my long business journey.

Thus, I became comfortable with sharing my opinions. I overcame the challenge by freely expressing my hardships to my networks. These included my clients, mentors, friends, and families. In every meeting, I would see if my networks faced similar challenges and note what others did to overcome them. As I shared my challenges, I realized that I was not alone in facing the hardships of lack of transparent business law and reliable consultants. I began to discuss the fees my consultants were charging and soon realized that they were outrageous.

I didn't freely express my shortcomings at first, but as I expanded my business networks and dealt with more people, they started to share their hardships. This opened a new door and made me feel comfortable sharing my own experiences. As I shared more of my shortcomings and hurdles, people started to recommend their networks of legal and tax consultants. After thorough analysis, I decided to hire a new consultant and quickly cut off ties with my old consultant

Did you change the way you conduct business after overcoming this tough time?

During the initial phases of starting my company, I focused on hiring and consulting people within my networks without thinking about their professional work or doing a proper background check. After I faced the hardship of trusting an unreliable legal and tax consultant, I started to make a habit of only focusing on contacting consultants through referrals. I changed my focus by only trusting people with a robust professional background or within my professional network.

Furthermore, I habitually asked more than one expert about the topic and compiled their fees. Similarly, I started to open up more about my hardships when sharing my company with others. I wore failure and challenge as a badge of honor rather than hiding them. I changed my perspective on failure and began asking questions about my hardships. For instance, I asked business owners whether they fulfilled their tax and legal obligations on time. I came across a few company owners unaware of specific business laws and rules, and I advised them to consult a professional consultant.

I also started researching legal obligations independently and questioned my new consultant if I had any doubts. We would often discuss how a particular problem could be solved and came to a fruitful conclusion which helped me to run my business more smoothly. Although I delegated the end tasks, I would also research the topic from my side.

Can you provide a word of wisdom for an entrepreneur facing a tough time in business?

Firstly, I advise anyone starting a business to hire people based on their professional background and work rather than solely based on a personal connection, even though they are friends or family. The best way to hire consultants or other professionals is through referral networks. Hiring them is a good idea if someone has been recommended based on solid references. Subsequently, we should ask questions to our referral networks about the person they recommend, whether they faced any challenges and how they solved them.

When starting a business, delegating tasks to others and focusing on our strengths are vital. However, even though we delegate the jobs, we should take responsibility and research to gain knowledge about the work ourselves. This way, we can openly discuss our ideas with the consultants or other professionals, so there are views of two people. Additionally, whenever we delegate the task to other professionals, we should also research the fees they are charging. It is always best to focus on the best offer rather than the cheapest.

Lastly, I advise anyone starting their own company to share their experiences with others. Starting a business is not easy, and even though it sounds fancy, it takes a lot of hard work. When we have the support and guidance of others, our ownership journey becomes a whole lot easier. Therefore, I advise others facing hardships in their business to start sharing more with their networks, which helps them connect with others and build relationships. Rather than being ashamed of the difficulties we face when starting our businesses, we should wear them like a badge and be proud that we overcame them. When we share the experiences of our hardships, others will get a chance to learn from us and not repeat the same mistake for which they will be forever grateful.

Going against the norm

Quratulain Aisha

I am a young entrepreneur with a dream of becoming a millionaire under twenty-five. I graduated with a degree in Software Engineering back in 2021. Currently, I am a freelancer and a business owner.

Growing up in a family where my father had a 9-5 job, it was difficult for us to plan family vacations or spend our precious moments of life with him. He was always busy with loads of work, and we never got to spend enough time with him.

Sometimes we did not have enough money to go out as his salary was fixed and our expenses were barely managed. All of this became the main motivation for me to start a freelance career, in which I would not be bound for some specific time with a fixed amount of salary. I wanted to enjoy the entire world with my family and always wished this for other people in my nation too.

I started my own educational institute, six months back, that focuses on teaching Pakistanis about freelancing and digital earning platforms. My only focus was to make Pakistani people advance in the field of technology and non-traditional ways to earn money. I wanted them to excel in this field to eradicate poverty, as many people graduate and still do not land any job, which is a major issue our country is currently facing.

I felt the need for a physical institute for people who are less able to understand educational online video content due to having little or no knowledge of using any digital platform or even a language barrier. Hence, I decided to provide a dedicated building and workspace with proper mentorship so that people may learn as if they were in some traditional Pakistani schools.

What was the toughest time in your business journey and what led up to this hardship?

Here in Pakistan, the concept of freelancing/online earning is not so common, and people still believe it to be a myth. Traditional methods of earning, like 9-5 jobs, are considered honorable. Among the biggest hardships I faced when I started my institute was that people did not show any positive response for months.

One time, a girl visited me to inquire about the subjects the institute offers. While I was telling her about the course outlines, she started laughing and said "I earn a handsome amount of salary from my traditional job, and everyone is busy with their jobs. Nobody will waste their time to learn such skills when they are already earning and are considered more honorable than freelancers."

To be honest, I was shocked by her response. I asked her about her "handsome" salary amount; she told me it was "forty-five thousand Pakistani rupees;" which is roughly $205. How could that be so handsome a salary to stop you from learning new opportunities in life and help you grow in the digital era? I still keep wondering about this.

The biggest hardship I faced is that people do not consider it worthy to grow and learn something out of the box. They still wish to have a 9-5 job routine, which at least guarantees them a salary at the end of the month. Simply, they do not want to take risks and avail themselves of opportunities that the world has to offer them.

Another big challenge I faced was that people here do not share their knowledge about non-traditional ways of earning with others. A lot of people are working as freelancers, but they never told their friends or others about their journey or experience as a freelancer. They think if they tell others, then others will snatch their opportunities from them. This attitude of other freelancers has developed an environment where people still do not know the importance of freelancing.

Traditional schooling systems here never teach such subjects in schools as they consider them to be worthless. People just do not want to make progress with a positive attitude. Handling such attitudes was one of the major challenges I had to face during my initial months.

Many people inquiring about the courses left the institute suggesting that I open a beauty parlor or restaurant to earn more from my business; as freelancing institutes like mine have no future and I have wasted my entire fortune on a worthless project.

How did you overcome this difficult time?

Coming up with a workable solution was another difficult step for me as I was challenging the attitudes of the people rather than some concrete physical problem. But eventually, I produced some good solutions.

To address the first hardship, about negative responses of people towards freelancing, I arranged a free seminar for people who were already earning from traditional jobs and offered them free food (Here in Pakistan, everyone shows a positive attitude towards free things). A lot of people came, and I showed them a full presentation of my success through freelancing. I arranged sessions with other freelancers to motivate them and show them the handsome salaries they were getting without any fixed working hours. The main motive of the seminar was fully focused on why freelancing is important and how it can change the lives of people in the future digital era. Thankfully, many people understood the importance of freelancing and how it could change their lives.

To overcome the second hardship of people not discussing their freelancing stories with others, I came up with the idea of arranging a contest, where people with the most interesting and inspiring success stories will win prizes. Thanks to that idea, many people participated and shared their journey inspiring others, thus becoming a motivation for them to start their journey as well.

To address the third hardship, I visited universities, academies, and educational institutes and offered them free 3-day training courses on how to start a freelance career. The content of the training was focused on how a student can earn enough money to support his daily necessities like pocket money or even partying with friends etc. There I introduced them to popular online freelancing sites, and other platforms where they can work and make money to support their financial needs.

I also requested the institutes to arrange some more sessions for students to learn more about non-traditional ways of earning and if possible, to try to add such subjects to the curriculum.

Did you change the way you conduct business after overcoming this tough time?

Previously my activities only involved teaching the courses I offered in my institute within my building premises. After realizing the fact that people in Pakistan need to understand the importance of freelance careers and have to change their attitudes towards it, I now also focus on letting people know about it as much as I can.

After the hardships I faced, I began arranging a free session every Saturday and Sunday for people who know nothing about online earning methods to teach them about freelancing. Along with this, I arrange consultation sessions with people who have tried to start a freelance career but failed due to a lack of mentorship.

I also made a group of inspiring freelancers with newbies so that they can discuss their journeys and how they started and how things are going now. This helps others to spread knowledge and lets others grow as well. I have made it mandatory for my students to share some part of the knowledge they learn in their sessions with their friends and family members and give me a brief report about it.

To be honest, I have seen a huge improvement in the attitudes and number of people enrolling in my institute to learn how to earn online. All of the people around me are now very positive and are willing to share the knowledge they have for others to grow as well. Although it is still small scale, with this approach I believe we can expand to the skies and beyond.

Can you provide a word of wisdom for an entrepreneur facing a tough time in business?

From my experience, I think the answer to negative attitudes is to ignore them completely and only follow one positive inspiration that has led you to start a business in the beginning. Never let others tell you what you should do. Always follow what you want to do and what you want to become.

It might be difficult for you at the start, but problems always come with their solutions. Look for the solutions and apply them to see what momentous results you can get. Try to find hidden opportunities in your problems, as they always lead to enormous success.

Also, try to seek help from others in your journey as the more people you have by your side the more chance you have to grow. Learn to grow and apply innovative ideas to your business that can help you in the long run.

Best of luck with your journeys ahead.

The Voice of Small Business: Tough Times

Afterword

I was absolutely awestruck with some of the stories presented through this book. The drive of these people to be successful definitely made an impression on me. I know that what I read was only a snapshot of the stories, but even that was enough to motivate me to work harder.

What struck me was that no matter where in the world, the struggles of people in small business are the same. The ups and the downs. Someone you know, or the business operator down the road might be going through the roughest patch in their lives at the moment.

A few years ago, I worked closely with a friend of mine, who for the sake of business, lost his home, and had to live at people's places and rely on their kindness. I have seen firsthand people go through tough times in business. It's not what I like to see, but I know tough times do come.

Are you going through a tough time at the moment? Being Laughed at? Out of cash? Not able to meet demand? Or maybe circumstances have made things tough for you at this point in time?

Take the stories that these 10 people that have been presented today. Draw strength from their experiences to overcome your troubles, so that one day your story will encourage many others.

The Voice of Small Business: Tough Times

We hope you enjoyed reading this book.
Explore the whole series by visiting
books.arthurlee.com.au

You can also get in touch with Arthur and explore his events by visiting

www.arthurlee.com.au

www.ingramcontent.com/pod-product-compliance
Lightning Source LLC
Chambersburg PA
CBHW050254220526
45465CB00002B/677